REEL TIME

PUBLISHED BY CREATIVE EDUCATION AND CREATIVE PAPERBACKS
P.O. BOX 227, MANKATO, MINNESOTA 56002
CREATIVE EDUCATION AND CREATIVE PAPERBACKS
ARE IMPRINTS OF THE CREATIVE COMPANY
WWW.THECREATIVECOMPANY.US

DESIGN AND PRODUCTION BY CHRISTINE VANDERBEEK
ART DIRECTION BY RITA MARSHALL
PRINTED IN THE UNITED STATES OF AMERICA

PHOTOGRAPHS BY ALAMY (IMAGEBROKER, NATURE PICTURE LIBRARY),
ISTOCKPHOTO (CHUNHAI CAO, CRISOD, DANBACHKRISTENSEN, GLOBALP,
MIHTIANDER, MOLOKO88, MPWOODIB, PHOTOGRAPHER3431, WILLARD),
SCIENCE SOURCE (ALVIN E. STAFFAN), SHUTTERSTOCK (JOHNNY ADOLPHSON,
DEEPSPACEDAVE, SERGEY GORUPPA, OLEKSANDR LYTVYNENKO, HAN MAOMIN,
NAPAT, PHOTOMASTER, KEITH PUBLICOVER, STEVENRUSSELLSMITHPHOTOS,
EVLAKHOV VALERIY, EDWARD WESTMACOTT, VADYM ZAITSEV), VEER (PILENS)

LIBRARY OF CONGRESS CATALOGING-IN-PUBLICATION DATA
ROSEN, MICHAEL J.
FRESH FISH / MICHAEL J. ROSEN.
P. CM. – (REEL TIME)
INCLUDES INDEX.
SUMMARY: A PRIMER ON THE BASIC DOS AND DON'TS OF FISHING, INCLUDING
TIPS ON WHERE TO FIND CERTAIN SPECIES, INFORMATION ON HOW A FISH'S
ANATOMICAL MAKEUP HELPS IT AVOID GETTING HOOKED, AND INSTRUCTIONS FOR
CLEANING A CATCH.

ISBN 978-1-60818-771-3 (HARDCOVER)
ISBN 978-1-62832-379-5 (PBK)
ISBN 978-1-56660-813-8 (EBOOK)
THIS TITLE HAS BEEN SUBMITTED FOR CIP PROCESSING UNDER LCCN 2016010298.

CCSS: RI.3.1, 2, 3, 4, 5, 7, 8, 10; RI.4.1, 2, 3, 4, 7, 10; RI.5.1, 2, 4, 10;
RF.3.3, 4; RF.4.3, 4; RF.5.3, 4

FIRST EDITION HC 9 8 7 6 5 4 3 2 1
FIRST EDITION PBK 9 8 7 6 5 4 3 2 1

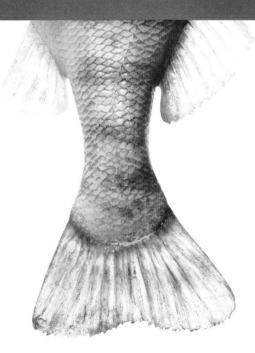

FRESH FISH

→ MICHAEL J. ROSEN ←

CREATIVE EDUCATION ⚓ CREATIVE PAPERBACKS

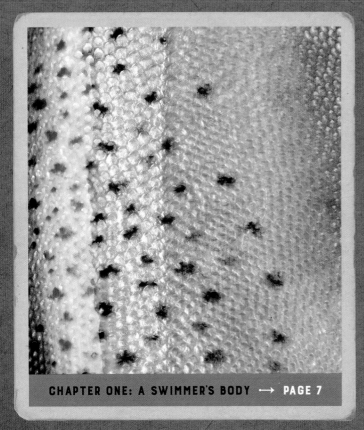

TABLE OF CONTENTS

A SWIMMER'S BODY

Most fish have seven or eight fins to help them maneuver through the water.

As you sit at the end of a dock, you spot a fish. While watching it swim in the current, you realize something: A fish's body was created for life in water. Most fish are pointed, long, and narrow. This streamlined shape allows fish to easily move through water.

A fish's tail is the caudal fin. It paddles from side to side, moving the fish forward. To go backward, a fish uses its pectoral and pelvic fins. These paired fins work together. They can move the fish forward, up, or down. They're also the brakes. A fish uses them to stop.

A fish has unpaired fins, too. The large, spiny fin running down its back is the dorsal fin. This stiff fin keeps the fish upright. Some fish also have an adipose fin. This small, soft fin is between the dorsal fin and the tail. Under a fish's belly is the anal fin. These fins help with braking and balancing.

A swim bladder helps fish rise and sink in the water. A fish pushes air into this organ. Like a bubble, it floats the fish upward. When the fish lets air out of its swim bladder, the bubble shrinks and the fish sinks.

Rows of scales cover the bodies of most fish. Only the face and fins are not covered. Scales protect against injury, parasites, and disease. A slimy coating adds further protection. It also helps the fish zip through the water.

FISH ANATOMY

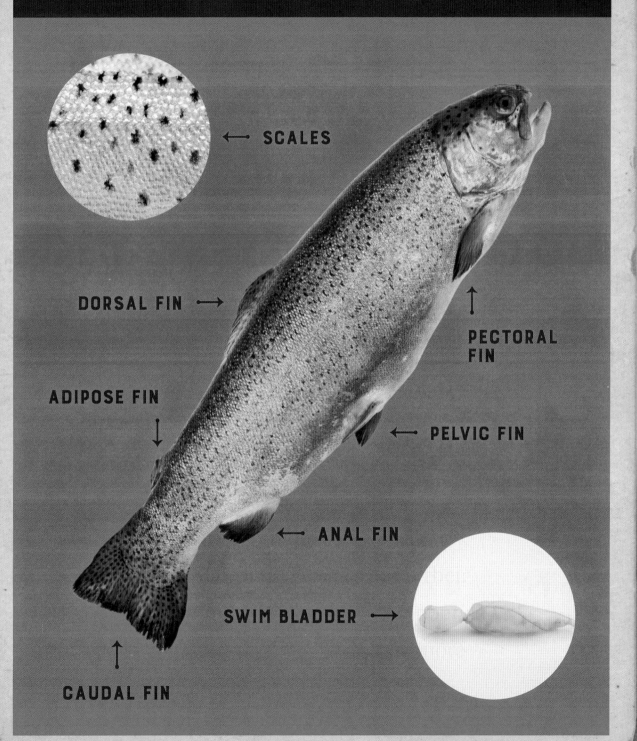

← SCALES

DORSAL FIN →

PECTORAL FIN ↑

ADIPOSE FIN ↓

← PELVIC FIN

← ANAL FIN

↑ CAUDAL FIN

SWIM BLADDER →

FRESH FISH → CHAPTER 2

LIFE AS A FISH

Under the gill cover, the gills are bright red, thanks to all the blood vessels they contain.

Like all living animals, fish breathe oxygen. However, a fish gets oxygen from water rather than air. It sucks water in through its mouth. Then it pushes the water out through its gills. The gills contain many tiny blood vessels. As water passes over them, the blood vessels take in oxygen.

Most animals stop growing when they reach their adult size. But fish continue to grow their entire life. So generally, the older the fish, the bigger the fish. Young fish eat plankton. As a fish grows, it eats larger foods. Some fish eat only plants. Some eat smaller fish. Others eat crabs or snails. Some kinds of larger fish may even eat frogs and salamanders!

Microscopic plankton

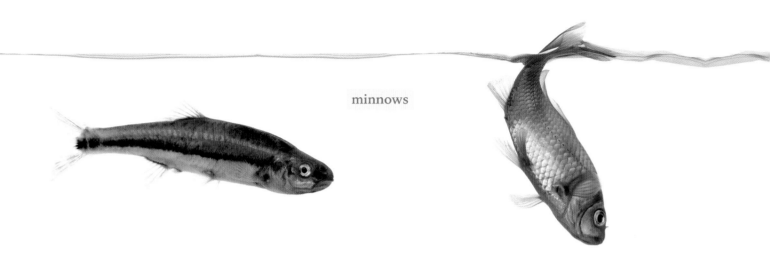

minnows

Some fish, such as bass and perch, have "teeth" in their throats. These aren't real teeth, but they help fish crush their food. Other fish have real—and really sharp— teeth. But even these fish don't chew! They use their teeth to grab and bite off food.

crayfish

Trout use their small, sharp teeth to grab and crush prey like minnows and crayfish.

FRESH FISH → CHAPTER 3

SENSING EVERYTHING

Fish's markings help them blend in with their surroundings and hide from predators.

Fish use their senses to survive. They find food and shelter through sight, smell, and sound. A fish's senses allow it to communicate with other fish and to avoid predators.

A fish can see several feet, especially in clear water. It can also see up into the air. Fish do not have eyelids. Even when a fish sleeps, its eyes are wide open.

A fish's nose is only for smelling. You can barely see the two nostrils. But they help the fish locate food. Some anglers use special scents to attract fish.

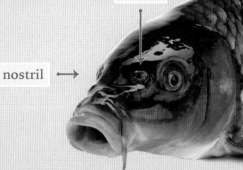

nostril

nostril →

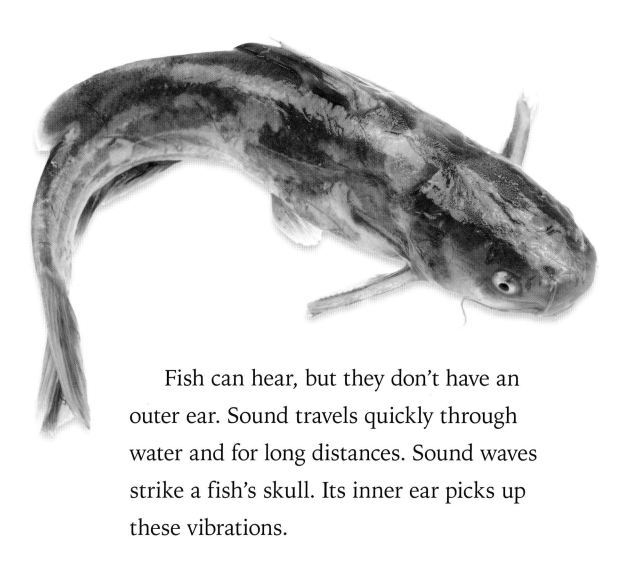

Fish can hear, but they don't have an outer ear. Sound travels quickly through water and for long distances. Sound waves strike a fish's skull. Its inner ear picks up these vibrations.

Some fish make sounds. A fish called a spot grunts. Croakers … *croak*! Other fish toot, whistle, burp, or squeak. But this is not speech. The "language" of fish is instinct: built-in knowledge and reactions. Fish "talk" through movement and color.

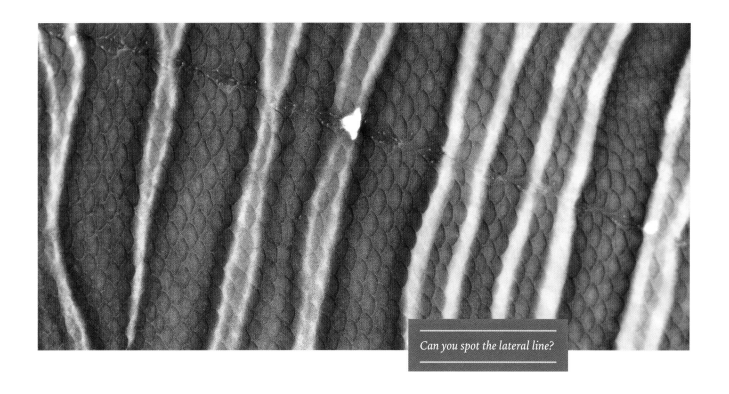

Can you spot the lateral line?

Fish don't have a sense of touch the way you and I think of it. But they do notice vibrations. A darker stripe runs down a fish's side. This lateral line half-feels and half-hears vibrations. It helps a fish find food, locate predators, and orient itself in currents. A fish also uses its lateral line to detect changes in water temperature and pressure.

FRESH FISH → CHAPTER 4

CATCH OF THE DAY

Crappies are small fish that prefer warm waters with lots of shelter.

Bluegill are small, flat fish. They have sharp dorsal fins and small mouths. Bluegill like warm, weedy waters with lots of food. They have two dark spots: one on the gill cover, the other on the dorsal fin.

Crappies (*CROP-eez*) average 6 to 12 inches (15.2–30.5 cm) in length. Most weigh between 8 and 16 ounces (227–454 g). The white crappie has dark bands on its back and sides. The black crappie has a rounder body.

Largemouth bass prefer shallow water with many places to hide. They have dark green backs that turn light green on their sides. They commonly weigh 2 to 5 pounds (0.9–2.3 kg), but the biggest can be more than 20 pounds (9.1 kg)!

Largemouth bass

Smallmouth bass

Yellow perch

Carp

Smallmouth bass are wary and good fighters. They love clear water and rocky, weedy shorelines. Brownish in color, some grow to be 24 inches (61 cm) long.

Yellow perch travel in large groups through slow rivers and wide ponds. If you catch one perch, you're likely to catch more. They are bright yellow with black bands.

Carp are big fish with large scales. They're olive green, fading to pale yellow

Catfish

Trout

on the belly. Carp have two small barbels. They are relatives of the common goldfish.

Catfish found in the United States include the yellow, brown, and black bullheads; the channel catfish; and the flathead catfish. All have barbels and a smooth, scaleless body.

Trout are enjoyed by many people for their taste, beauty, and cleverness. They are especially plentiful in the Great Lakes and streams in the western U.S. Wherever you are, you will likely find fresh fish to catch!

ACTIVITY: CLEANING YOUR CATCH

IF YOU DECIDE TO KEEP YOUR CATCH TO EAT, CLEAN IT THE SAME DAY YOU CAUGHT IT.

Cleaning fish can be messy, so it's best to do it outdoors. It also requires a sharp knife, so ask an adult to help you the first few times. If your fish doesn't have scales, skip to step 2.

MATERIALS

- old newspaper
- dull knife or spoon
- sharp knife

1 Wet the fish. Lay it down on a flat surface. Use a dull knife or spoon to scrape off the scales. Start at the tail, and scrape against the scales, toward the head. Rinse the fish and your hands to get rid of the scales.

2 Place the fish on top of several layers of newspaper. Use a sharp knife to slit the belly open. The cut doesn't need to be deep. Using the knife or a gloved hand, scrape out the fish's insides. Only the lining surrounding the fish's ribs and backbone should be left.

3 Slit the membrane that covers the backbone and remove the blood vessel found there.

4 Use a sharp knife to remove the head, tail, and fins. Rinse the fish well.

5 Wrap the newspaper around the discarded parts. Throw it away. Prepare the fish according to your favorite recipe. Enjoy!

anglers → people who fish

barbels → thick, whisker-like projections growing from a fish's mouth; barbels are covered with taste buds

current → the direction in which a body of water is moving

lateral line → the darker line that is a sensory organ running along a fish's body

parasites → organisms that live on or inside a fish and cause disease or death

plankton → small plants and animals that float in water and are not visible to the human eye

streamlined → having a smooth shape that moves forward with very little resistance

READ MORE

Levine, Michelle. *Fish*. Mankato, Minn.: Amicus, 2015.

Parker, Steve. *Fish*. New York: DK, 2005.

WEBSITES

Fishing Tips Depot

http://www.fishingtipsdepot.com/

Find fishing tips by species, technique, and type.

KidsBiology.com: Animal Database

http://www.kidsbiology.com/animals-for-children .php?category=Fresh%20Water%20Fish

Find out more about freshwater fish.

Note: Every effort has been made to ensure that the websites listed above are suitable for children, that they have educational value, and that they contain no inappropriate material. However, because of the nature of the Internet, it is impossible to guarantee that these sites will remain active indefinitely or that their contents will not be altered.

INDEX